The Pajamaist

9/06

DEMCO

Books by Matthew Zapruder

American Linden
The Pajamaist

The Pajamaist

Matthew Zapruder

COPPER CANYON PRESS

Printed in the United States of America

Cover art: Artist unknown, photograph, 2⅜ x 4 inches.

Copper Canyon Press is in residence at Fort Worden State Park in Port Townsend, Washington, under the auspices of Centrum Foundation. Centrum is a gathering place for artists and creative thinkers from around the world, students of all ages and backgrounds, and audiences seeking extraordinary cultural enrichment.

LIBRARY OF CONGRESS CATALOGING-IN-PUBLICATION DATA

Zapruder, Matthew, 1967–
  The pajamaist / Matthew Zapruder.
    p. cm.
  ISBN 1-55659-244-2 (pbk. : alk. paper)
  1. Title.
  PS3626.A67P35 2006
  811'.6—dc22

                                        2006010374

98765432 first printing

COPPER CANYON PRESS
Post Office Box 271
Port Townsend, Washington 98368
WWW.COPPERCANYONPRESS.ORG

Acknowledgments

Many thanks to the editors of the following publications where poems from this book first appeared: *Alaska Quarterly Review, Bomb, Boston Review, The Canary, Columbia: A Journal of Literature and Art, Electronic Poetry Review, Fence, The New Republic, New York Quarterly, NC2, Open City,* and *Swerve.*

"Dream Job" appeared in the 2006 poetry day calendar published by Alhambra Publishing in Brussels, Belgium. "Canada" was included in the anthology *Legitimate Dangers: American Poets of the New Century* (Sarabande, 2006). "The Pajamaist" first appeared in *Open City* magazine and was reprinted in the anthology *Awake! A Reader for the Sleepless* (Soft Skull, 2006).

Contents

I

Dream Job

Today abstracted
as a glass of milk
forgotten by a kid who went
into this interminable
rain to play, I was reading
up on the science of tracking
the movement of birds
through spring. It seems
just as for us says Professor
Martin Wikelski of Princeton
who each night for six weeks
with his team of researchers
captured and carefully
injected thrushes with double-
labeled water ampules,
for the birds a long
spring flight is painless
relative to the fighting
at rest areas that can really
drain the migrating out of you.
I have so many questions.
First the doubly labeled
water technique. If on
a cool day a bird at rest
a nonflying bird
staying warm consumes
the same kilojoules
as two-and-a-half
wind tunnel hours,
how many isotopes
does it take to tremble

in the researcher's hand?
What happens if overhead
in the clouds or laughing
at a joke about penguins
someone loses the birds?
Each morning the researchers
inject a small
portion of double water,
each evening
the blood reports,
to where they are going
the thrushes move closer,
the researchers follow,
soon they can go
back to Princeton
Twin Rivers or Hightstown,
say goodbye thrushes,
and it occurs
to me in my snow globe
surrounded with rain
on Water Street by the sea,
it's possible all this
capturing daily
was for some other purpose.
Put down the paper.
I'm sure I can see
each week the team
growing increasingly
tender holding
the small thrushes they
probably had to name.
Go, Jerry, soon you will be
in Canada where
Neil Young was born.

Thank You for Being You

Poetry begins here. Brand-new summer
faces the academy of youth. Gold
division buys gold. Everybody grew up
in a subculture, overcoming presentation.
Explosive subjectivity, anxiety loops,
available light digging Manhattan.
When things sound alike, does it
make them sisters? Come dancing
bitter city, it's only natural.
Carousel with its horses removed,
suddenly I don't feel so abandoned.
I want to communicate with you,
I'm trying as hard as a human,
but the white space always stops
me. When they found him he was
holding a shovel. When I loved
you all afternoon, you were absent,
the neighbors woken, your cries
were the actual miracle. Defeated,
I tell endless bedtime stories, bounce
off others, understand power.
Even feedback can be helpful. Move
the radio to a slightly bigger
basement where it won't be too proud.
Restless spirit, it's you. You
are family, you are dark mysterious
helpful time for time to pull
in a little, curl up with some reasons,
and shut out the world.

First Time, Long Time

Those big oily birds cleaning
their feathers on the roof,
what are they called? The
radio crackles. All over
the city installations open
their white walls to greet us
with mystification. Blind
the grey arthritic cat leans
his clouded head on his paw
waiting for footsteps. Wind
plays the chime. How
can it be the first and last
time all at once? The old
woman hobbled out of
the school bus. So much
sun, dead middle of summer,
worse than it's ever been. I love
baseball, it makes me angry
and hopeful for justice.
I once rode a boat all night
past the dark islands,
my fingers were playing
a tiny violin everyone heard,
no one knew what it was,
they thought a music box
in the luggage had opened.
I remember holding a coin,
but not why I said I too
see the lights of Tunisia,
Brooklyn, Spain, it took

ages to cross three avenues
through the morning
to where I could sit
down like an American
and start writing this for you.

The Lark

O green rolling mind of the hills

the telephone is raining

a little carved of late morning
shed
where a little blond body

behind an opaque white curtain fails

inside it
      to translate
            rain and grey

into something useless enough
to be useful

to the fable drinker
in the park
that's me

thinking some people
in the park when they run
      through me look

         like they've always
      been glad to be running
from something.

Others seem
      to have just gotten up

from placidly keeping
bees in a structure

    built of the feeling
    they should be feeling

a need to leave the valley.

Last night some hazy conversation
drifted
down the careless hall to wake

the newlyweds inside me.

    Let them never make a sound.
    Let them be closed

until they open
    their eyes
    at the same time

and try on old hats in silence.

Is that what they do

said the little blond body to the fable drinker

here try on old rain
inside me in silence

try on not trying
on that old radiant silence

try on a longing
for music not to be used

just take
          two steps into

          the o useless
around the ancient mountain revolution

that it may gather
a few kilowatts
of your wanting inside it

for the king
          who sleeps

to keep him warm

and grow
his beard for power.

O take off your solemn
          head and bang
          a little
music for longing

          not to be any sort of ship that sails

anyone into the ocean
inside him of you know this rain
is for us no longer.

You know
        sadness hurts
        because music

actually right now

in a valley
of differential green
recalcitrant sadness

inside you hurts.

You know you drink
        too much night

        and you say O night

you drank too much
                homemade night

          some death wish
          daughter from a bunch of mother

resembling gestures concocted
and woke
still inside me

        thinking I'm night

        before remembering

I'm a sweet
green balcony morning over

the market breathing people.

O rain of a birthday present
wrapped in argument
over yesterday's
literary supplement

I follow you
      deeper   inside
      the town of you know

      how to be
          caring and not caring

down the hall
at 4 a.m. from two you loved
     failing to be quiet

O caring and not caring outside me quiet

pass me the green hat
with a feather in it

O feather falling in love with the world

There Is a Light

Whenever behind your windows I look
from my balcony down at you you are open,
at any hour among the pyramids
of eggplant and whiskey albanian shadows
drag their shadows, I could watch
this shadow clock for hours and do,
it is timing me, and each time your doors
part my lips hydraulical
silently clatter o solemn untamed
maternal albanian market why
at this fucked time of night are you open
locked within yourself and asking
the same thing of me, small
leaning over the balcony figure watching
your painless hydraulic scar
from both sides open releasing silence,
in silence you have been here
forever since 1993, you assure me
with your calm ancient terror,
you force a man who looks on you
to doubt his sleep and lack
of sleep, o most magnificent
pregnant man, you give birth to things
surrounded with chocolate
and things with chocolate buried
inside them, you give birth to pine-
scented dishwashing fluids, you give
birth to placenta which some people eat,
you give birth to etcetera's
every pleasure in every hour,

o low market wearing the naked dress
of windows lettered with emerald
translucent letters, what pale
green inside me memory dress
now gives birth to the story of you
giving birth to the story of me
giving birth to my awe of you
at 3 a.m. giving birth to a mother
of her sleeping children young and free
who with pale green arabic music
leaking from one of her earrings
looks up with her gaze and unlocks me
then turns into her drifting toward
the opposite and therefore holy direction

Canada

By Canada I have always been fascinated.
All that snow and acquiescing.
All that emptiness, all those butterflies
marshaled into an army of peace.
Moving north away from me
Canada has no border, away
like the state its northern border
withers into the skydome. In a world
full of mistrust and self-medication
I have always hated Canada.
It makes me feel like I'm shouting
at a child for letting a handful
of pine needles run through his fist.
Canada gets along with everyone
while I hang, a dark cloud
above the schoolyard. I know
we need war, all the skirmishes
to keep our borders where
we have placed them, all
the migration, all the difference.
Just like Canada the Dalai Lama
is now in Canada, and everyone
is fascinated. When they come
to visit me, no one ever leaves me
saying, the most touching thing
about him is he's so human.
Or, I was really glad to hear
so many positive ideas regardless
of the consequences expressed.
Or I could drink a case of you.

No one has ever pedaled
every inch of thousands of roads
through me to raise awareness
for my struggle for autonomy.
I have pity but no respect for others,
which is not compassion, just ordinary
love based on attitudes toward myself.
I wonder how long I can endure.
In Canada the leaves are falling.
When they do each one rustles
maybe to the white-tailed deer
of sadness, and it's clear
that whole country does not exist
to make me feel crappy
like a candelabra hanging
above the prison world,
condemned to freely glow.

Haiku

Yesterday for you
I wrote a poem so full
of lies it woke me
stunned like someone
bitten in the middle of the night
or a bird that just
smashed into a very clean window.
Now it's so early
it's still night
and this time I'm hardly
trying at all, holding carefully
in my palms
the knowledge that
I don't know anything about you.
And how could you know
mosquitoes love my blood
because it's full
of something they love,
or that I like to play chess
in the morning
with a serbo-croatic book,
never getting any better?
Or that to drink
seltzer with lemon in the dark
thinking of Isamu Noguchi
calms me, but only sometimes?
How I'm a blue
vial of delusions.
How on my biceps
I have a star that never

aches when I tell the truth.
How I'm always
in love with someone
I'll never meet (see,
I can't put three words
together without lying!).
And all the things
about you I don't know,
which is everything.
Did you never
want to be a dancer?
Were your ankles
too thin, and you didn't
even know it?
Did you love
or were you afraid
of horses (one threw me
when I was a child)?
Did your mother show you
how to wrap a towel
around your wet hair
like an arab queen,
or did you just know
how to paint your nails and hold
the telephone like that
between your chin
and shoulder?
The color of your eyes.
Do they change
on a bridge?
When you lie?
It feels so good
to be clear, and free,

not like a buddhist
or a haiku but just sort of
dumb, hardly able
in the middle of night
to speak. Only
enough to say
thank you for the cake,
how it came
wrapped in tinfoil,
newborn, almost
as sweet as the thought
of you thinking
a moment of me.
Most things come
by time and circumstance
separated, waiting
to be repaired.
But not that cake
which I ate
quickly, like
it was about to disappear.
Let's start again.
I don't think
that's a bird out there,
it sounds more like
a person trying
to sound like a bird.
Or maybe a bird a person
didn't mean
but still taught
how to whistle.
You keep sleeping
and I'll stop trying

to decide if it's better
to change other people
or how they see us,
or what's more
urgent and futile,
to unlock
or to invent the past.

II

Twenty Poems for Noelle

Noelle, somewhere in an apartment
symphony number two
listens to you breathing.
Broken glass in the street.
What was once unglowing glows.
Through tiny holes the page
exhales, fire escape white in the sun,
and vaguely parasitic
cramped in the courtyard
endlessly undulate the leaves.
Silos preside over thousands of miles.
Tiny puffs move the flags.
The child of the happiest woman
died and who will save us?
It's good to end something never begun,
but the question always is. Static
in the trees. People in their clothes.
Empty tables facing the street
in open verandas, wait for beautiful
women, they always come.

Summer's breathing, and these
Noelle are only for you.
I don't care if you need them,
or if you're happy right now, just
dream toward a little calm
something other than medicine
brings. It's too hard to keep
imagining beyond. What happens
if all its little boats into sunset
disappear leaving only that
leaving feeling? Current events
don't harm the radio. Great unions,
slow down to move quicker.
Summer's a sketchbook, and what
doesn't lead us further is otherwise
known as nothing. You loathe it too.
Someone told me never to write,
I was too much of a fitter, but
I think he couldn't see the sloshing
oceanic lack of calm I bring to the medium.

In the sketchbook terrible drawings
of my hand, grotesque hairs,
all seen with eyes Noelle
that couldn't even tell you the color
of the house in Minneapolis.
But that's not why I left.
I left because is it so wrong
if I'm going to die to want
to do so in a city with at least
one excellent delicatessen
and the proximity of you?
Thunder over the stadium.
Tens of thousands of eyes regard
the plane becoming suddenly
sinister in lazy circles
then safe again. They are trying
to scare us and what will we do
when with actual tears they come
to inform us paintings have been
real and our masters all along?

Independence day, the sky
on high alert, you look
like you hear colors
Noelle over the rooftops bursting,
on the ledge of a holiday
it's good to be lonely,
people act that way
on the street when their team
spectacularly has fallen
holding its shin or some
thing you get for winning
something european, with joy
greeks sob and latins gnash
their garments and fall
down in a beautiful tantrum
the city parentally ignores,
we're afraid, are they listening,
I say the more diligently
they fuck with us
the more american we get.

He threw a gem. The sidewalks
shimmered a little with heat
and a little with glee. Weathermen
and astronauts rattle on
about the sky. Noelle remember
Guy Lafleur skating through
the radio under the sheets?
Not like wind, more like
murmuration. Digital
numbers green to read by.
Nine victories, right
on time to the party
trying to moonwalk
I excruciated the disco.
Those Canadiens, though,
they never lose to anyone,
not even themselves, in their
even relentless grace
they look up once in a while
and run out of time.

The fortune-teller's room
glows a little golden as if
the future sunset she describes
fills it and I see the wildness
that fears nothing.
Noelle are you on a carpet
lying with your head
slightly turned upward
toward a voice that says
I have painted the sky exactly
the color that it is? The guitars
chime. The swingset
swings in the wind.
Multicolored cross
on the neck of a stranger,
you hang in that lovely
way we do until no one
watches us turn away
from the rearview. Tiny
the figure waves in the distance.

What does not change is my t-shirt
for three days and the will
to check e-mail. Today I must
enter the comic book convention
with funeral in my eyes. When
I knocked the guitar off the bed
it made a brutal clanging Noelle
would have loved. Check for
antique cracks. The stove
leaking gas all down the hallway
and up through the skylight.
A man blew soap bubbles
onto the gasket. Thirteen
years old and already no
longer a dirtbiker. Jersey
City fills with halters safely
into each other careening
and love requited while
russian painters discuss
the technique of rain.

O nervous Harlem drivers
passing the quiet wedding
the stadium shining in the sun
this was the clicking year
cicadas shaking the trees
the sound of terror
their blind red eyes
Noelle careen them toward each other
ciphers floating through the air
dried golden wings
everyone checking their hair
the swollen birds
moving drunk across the lawns
graduation time again
no matter how many hours in dowry
who can marry the dark
Nina in the bathroom writing
too late to die in each other's arms
no matter how many friends
sometimes they are sad or asleep

The car alarm has a blinking
indicator that will not cease,
next to Tompkins Square
Park people suggest
we disconnect
what's disconnected,
helpless the power
runs onto the street,
Noelle I am drained,
so many things, all of them
stupid, what personality
endless under the big
smile can suffer,
does wildness help, does
being like a piece
of paper blown and lifting
upward, suddenly limbs
have been light
translucent branches of
a tree in the wind all along.

Night, one hears sounds
under the pavement,
something is always
being repaired, under
the red painted table
that Aztec Camera
tape lies where it fell,
its label with drawings
in pencil of little flowers,
Noelle were you ever cool,
that is aware that somehow
not to be aware is the only
lasting form of awareness,
you live in Brooklyn,
a green hexagon floats
above your head, now
everyone sees it, my problem
is I would like there to be
some kind of preferably
gentle sorting without me.

Opera pouring from the tenement,
dark sobbing into the light.
Callas drinking absinthe
under an assumed name
in Toulon then singing
calypso for sailors asleep
in a basement. Those
great songs are not our songs.
Songs we know crown us
like flowers. Songs of the past
Noelle their white walls
all around me return
gold sounds big clean amps
once chimed so sad and transistor,
machines played drums, it was
the fashion now distant
and cold enough to trouble
the ghost in you still riding your bike
under pink hi fidelity thunder.

Houses with skylights make
the most of sunshine. As a child
who isn't lost in dreaming?
Forensic laboratories
for examining the dark materials
flower quietly in low-slung
suburban pastel buildings.
Like a scroll that hung once
in a palace we have a relationship
to power. Solace and wonder.
Remember the clouds, the massive white
ones tinged with pink Noelle
and hanging disturbingly across
the horizon? Down the hill
on the corner where the bus always
came too late a defeater
waited in the bushes with
talcum and a cardboard dagger
about to assassinate me
in a game I kept agreeing to play.

*　*　*

Gauzy white curtains
blow when there isn't a breeze.
The chandelier hangs. Twelve
silver spheres reflect twelve
reflections. Candles
shaped like faces. The ghosts
can't stand a locked door,
they want you to climb
into the lost domain for another
picnic on the island.
Clear the mind of particles.
The merits of not being a sculpture
Noelle seem less important
than ones of moving, for bodies
follow shadows they cast
and shadows follow whatever
instructs them and the blue women
can no longer instruct
though their voices still make
a beautiful troubling.

There's a little medicine
it calibrates deficient blood
so many tiny devices
cure so many new diseases
constantly along the streets
shedding skin we breathe
bits of skin move in the lungs
the streets somewhat neglected
feel too often they are mentioned
in polemics dressed as concern
for arab masses and not enough
in ones about how no dress
she wears along them is ever
boring Noelle but intermittent
like thunder moves or it's sunny
on both boroughs and we feel
better already lost camera
having the time of our lives
please return to report we're
having the time of our lives

A glass of wine with Marie in the garden
olives   interior space   the old
distressed sign said grand hotel
de la russe and we were entrusted
to a ghost in black   o that false
welcome left bank feeling
beyond the gate Brooklyn awake
Jennifer in an antique skirt
buying a dress   lucky window
the telephone down the stairs not ringing
bad news bad news in my sleep
knot of anxiousness vs. the medicine
all the friends times all the things
they do times all the possibilities
Noelle only talking disperses
nothing better than quiet talking
in the garden with Marie
and the ghost while down under
manhattan bridge overpass the rich
carefully lick each other in their lofts

✳ ✳ ✳

Maryland I can tell you was
no heaven, more like a context
where either the death throes
of winter were constantly rattling,
or summer's profusion of examples
stunned a child of privilege
living in a neighborhood of hostile
catholic houses salvaged
from America's ambiguous
racial history. When I looked
in the mirror I never once saw
one surface, or a 20th century
master of sampling, just someone
acting as if everything is related
or could be a test. So let's
Noelle never finish passing
through the clerestory marvels
in the dream room of the past
except for quick escapes
into the future, without a map.

* * *

Beautiful plagiarist, come
to me slowly. The day
wears a series of windows.
The day wears a veil.
Ukrainian church
full of tiny wood crosses,
nobody knows the whole city.
Surrounded by motherfuckers,
a boy slaps a red handball.
Clack the chess piece
and bright noise spreads
out over the reader.
Evening on both sides
of the river, boats moving
through it, on the way
to the modern hotel she
stumbled Noelle, blood
on her knee, touching her
felt so full of that antique
climbing a hill kind of feeling.

Who knows where
the sparrow falls?
All day that song,
the dead one's light
body pushed along
the street in my head.
Through the floating
gardens of Xochimilco
painted boats carry
tourists carrying flowers.
I hear the singing.
Where are we going?
So beautifully naive
intellectuals meet
where intellectuals meet.
Among the girders
giant time flowers
flowered Noelle,
and like a weblog
I thought of Oaxaca.

Dream of climbing a hill,
and wake to everything
telling a story. Grief
a black shoe, or
a yellow leaf stuck
to it moving through
the city. The city
an empty envelope filling
with news. The day
a golden city changing
very slightly the name
of its hospital. The feeling
twilight fills everyone
and still beautiful they look
up the skirt of the
night sky. The name
that means little caress
I fell asleep in. Yes
Noelle that's what they
call multiple starlings.

Over the meadow
glides the wind.
Wind like a hand.
Waves you can see.
Left behind we
struggle through all
our noisy troubles
to love what's without
us continued. Joy
I've failed myself
and will with all possible
speed come to you.
To think of us as grasses.
What a drag. Some say
it's a sphere with rivers
of blood and lying, but
what I say is it's a giant
opus breathing you're
wrong if you ever say
Noelle said no more dying.

The Pajamaist

In my dream, I was writing a novel called The Pajamaist.

There had been a marked advance in the field of suffering.
Researchers in the Institute For The Advancement Of
Reduction Of Suffering had discovered it could be trans-
ferred, painlessly, from one subject to another. What did
this mean in practical terms? No one had to suffer any
longer, at least not for free!

We had only to sleep in each other's pajamas, or take some
kind of pill to supplement the pajama-switching. I hadn't
yet dreamed this out.

The first and greatest of all the sufferers was the
Pajamaist, an unemployed white whale in his midthirties. I
mean male.

When I sleep I don't wear pajamas. I prefer to sleep naked,
and thrash the bedsheets around until they wrap me in a
protective covering with only my head and feet exposed.
Each of my sleeping partners has added to the catalogue
of possible means of exhibiting displeasure with this
nightly process, yet suspiciously, not one has ever thought
to buy me pajamas.

Maybe they think pajamas would make me resemble a float
in the annual Sleep Parade.

Well there should be.

Once I bought a pair of white silk pajamas, it ended badly.

The Pajamaist had been privately operating as a sufferer, nights and weekends for a few friends and relatives, who in their days and nights began to exhibit such characteristics of a totally suffer-free existence that Researchers from the Institute began to notice weird spikes in their suffer graphs, and hired an Investigator.

The Investigator took the Suffer Location Graphs into the city and began to search for the spike sources, radiating so obviously through their days (and incidentally creating new and additional alienation suffering in the coworkers, wives, and ex-girlfriends surrounding them that there is to this day some quiet speculation in the corners that, like matter in the universe or total weight within a nuclear family unit, suffering has an immutable quotient and can never be reduced, only transferred) that it was easy to trace these rays of suffer-free happiness back from the subjects to their common source, a tiny impossibly black dot of suffering.

Tracing back the suffer location rays to an apartment near the center of the unnamed city, the Investigator took a room across the street and watched through black plastic binoculars he had been given on one of his early birthdays so that he could when taken to the arena more clearly see the successes of his invincible team, whose name had been recently changed at the insistence of the city fathers.

Sleeping, at first the Pajamaist looked peaceful. Then began the Throes, they were horrible to watch and produced great suffering in the one who was watching. Therefore, instinctively, in order to shield the watcher from

further suffering the Pajamaist isolated himself, a proce-
dure quickly coded as part of the Suffer Transfer Protocol
so as not to merely spread out in a thin, at first unde-
tectable, but ultimately equally palpable over a longer
period of time layer, but actually to reduce the Total
Quantity Of Suffering in the world. For one can easily see
how observing the Throes of the Pajamaist must render in
the watcher new suffering, and fail to reduce anything.

Long after the histories of the period had been exhaus-
tively written, a secret minority of revisionists gathered in
silence to theorize this self-imposed isolation was in itself
the necessary and sufficient key to the Suffer Transfer
Protocol. The Pill was totally unnecessary, and one could
achieve the same effect in free communities just large
enough to permit their own isolation protocols surround-
ing the general principle of isolation of the Object. In my
dream we lost contact, and believe they were somehow
overheard, or eaten.

The Investigator further noted that in the course of his
observations (and especially at night when he should have
been sleeping) he had divined in the Throes nine varieties
of suffering in addition to the tenth, the Purely Physical:
suffering that others suffer less than you; suffering that oth-
ers suffer more than you; suffering that there is suffering at
all; suffering for "no reason"; suffering that there can be
suffering for "no reason"; suffering that there are logical
connections but no god or vice versa; suffering that you
have in the past suffered and thus "wasted time"; suffering
that you will again in the future suffer and thus "waste
time"; and suffering that those you love have, are, or will in
the future suffer from any and all of the varieties.

Independently the Researchers had come exactly to this Categorization System, but, fearing the Investigator would in his newfound boldness go found a Competing Institute, diagnosed him as borderline schizomniac anal-suppressive and suggested an Eastern Treatment.

Or more accurate, found yet another Competing Institute, for in addition to the Institute For The Advancement Of Reduction Of Suffering there was the Institute To Speculate On Theories Of Suffer Reduction. In this Institute were gathered the ex-girlfriends, mensheviks, priests, standardized testers, and other remnant heirs to the ragtag opposition to the end of the era of randomly allocated suffering, those who both proclaimed and believed that while suffering could not actually be transferred or reduced, one could speculate on the matter, and arrive through the glory of abstract mathematics at a theoretical solution to the "Problem of Suffering."

With the advent of the Pill, the latter Institute began to suffer from a serious lack of Funding, and no longer figures in the dream.

The Pill is small and blue, and contains within it one specklet of a substance that cannot without violating certain totally proprietary events be very accurately described. In my dream it was called either The Small Blue, The Small Blue Vehicle, or Pajama's Little Helper.

Wearing the pajamas of a soon-to-be Former Sufferer, by ingesting The Small Blue Vehicle the professional Sufferer is in a secret and as far as the Non-Profit Institute is concerned totally proprietary way open to the suffering of the original sufferer as transferred through physical droplets, night sweats, the essence of palpitations connected directly to the most concentrated form of suffering, in sleep.

True, suffering that occurs in waking is more surprisingly painful, especially in the morning, when a Waker feels mocked and betrayed by the very fact of day. One could very well even call consciousness openness to the possibility of hurt, though one hesitates to light the headlamp and trundle off deeper into that forest of rue.

Nevertheless, the pain of this conscious suffering (which occurs at a time of waking, or relative awareness, or daylight) is in no way correspondent to the *concentration* of suffering, which is at its highest potency during the first hours of sleep. We just think suffering hurts less in sleep because we are sleeping. In our own nightmare throes, we excrete the suffering, and though more exhausted wake purified and ready for day. But an excess of suffering cannot be fully excreted in sleep, and accumulates, accreting.

This, by the way, is why insomniacs, otherwise known as Pure Subjects, have such an aspect of deprivation and suffering, never having a natural opportunity in sleep to excrete it.

I am not, nor have I ever been, an insomniac. I sleep like a baby, albeit a very agitated one. I am the eldest of countless children, and therefore received exactly my share of attention, enough to ensure in me from toddlerhood to the present a gentle, non-geometric increase in smile frequency well within melancholia parameters.

It occurs to me now that watching someone else suffer, or even waiting in a different white room designed for

Subjects where I could not see the Sufferer but know he suffered for me, would in and of itself constitute suffering, so there would have to arise in my dream some kind of solution. Such a solution could be so horrible that I am tempted to cease thinking of this mechanism any further.

Yet here I can imagine the Pajamaist, suffering quietly and unobserved in his room, asleep in some ways, awake in so many others. I feel for him not suffering, but the kind of pleasurable yet very real sorrow I feel only in my dream life, where the bright colored objects of pre-cognition someone is quietly encouraging me to fit together keep falling from a very high table, and the first words I learn to speak are I'm sorry, I realize this is important to you, but it just seems like a bit too much trouble, this fitting together, and anyway I get confused.

IV

January

The small cities touch each other with snow.
There's no any longer to miss, only this shadow
phonograph still running its shadow needle
over and over that after-the-record static,
making an aftersound cave I love to sit in
and listen to part of me scaring that part of me
willing to crawl just a bit farther out onto
the sound of ice long after I hear it cracking.
For a time in January letters to pharmaceutical
companies didn't seem even a little contrived,
I was genuine and grateful and wanted
to thank them for I thought I could hear
them saying thank you and though you may
for weeks feel a frozen lake on a public access
station inside you reading a list
of cloud cancellations, the window will turn
surely neutral, shortly you will begin to bump
as if with helium filled along from room
to room, picking up and holding you to your ear,
saying you sound like a program
about calm parts of the ocean caught
by bunny ears loosed from a seventies zenith.
You sound like you think by rhythmically limping
to help the empty apartment below
compose an overture to a symphony known
as science of eluding. Nobody wanders
along the strings. In such a thought
one could be beautiful, like a ballet
starring a naked but for a half-dressed in pink
tulle she once wore mirror holding

a shard of spring. During reacclimation to time
we recommend you keep on doing that
science of eluding thing, don't look too hard
for the manual, allow some things to leave you
unfinished, walk on leaking, stray, always
a left behind bird sleeps on the science
of patience shall always elude you wire.
Is that you? Some trees we have built
cast meaningful shadows, they misinform you
warnings from the other side of the veil
will if you do just a little more good than
you're able be brought you. You are a coast
that drifts toward able to wake
to holding those one or two moments
she let you sleep in her lap.
Those one or two moments january me now,
but only for one or two moments.

Tonight You'll Be Able

It may feel good to go wherever.
Desires lead you into old familiar
destructive awareness. Going a thousand
miles away seems to be keeping up.
Unsettled and anxious signals:
they're so microscope. Be a sleuth.
Tiny sparkling under those around you
sees you feeling and waiting. Life
today is slow-moving coworkers.
Respond by giving your profile
a new sense of clarity, and feel
ready to share your outlook even
if they may not be as excited. It
makes you good to spread your joy.
People, it's harder to be yourself.
A series of role-playing opportunities
appeases, showing the authentic
you won't hurt anything. Focus
on your lovely find that there
are many more things. Tonight,
you'll be able to talk to anyone
about anything, make all the loved ones
muster up, chat with character,
keep alive the conversations.
You feel you're getting something
someone gives you. The key
to a series of coincidences you
play matchmaker to. An odd couple,
the present you and the future
in a big suit, a new haircut,

or, better than anticipated, funds.
A few minor changes to June.
Love partners, your lucky numbers
are 4, 7, 18, 21, and 32. Ask yourself
what would I do if I knew I could
not fail.

Water Street

Yesterday afternoon I woke
    with a giant like a skydome

        full of nothing but laughter

            emptiness in my mouth.
            My mouth a laughing
                factory

generating funerals
        memories and instructions.

            Little chip in the light blue plastic
                rimmed with artificial gold

            base of the snow globe
                  must I do

            what the ghosts cannot?

            That is go
out into the world

                  in search of some epoxy.

                Stay in the moment, do not wander.

                Turning it upside down melted snow
                  through the cracked

            sky above the little version

of the town of Providence

runs onto
the blue
notebook with a dragonfly
etched in darker
blue on the cover.

My window

lets in I'm not happy
and I'm not
sad chimes

from the radio
the roofers listen to.

Above the streets
little leaves
wait for the key to turn.

Out into static
voices

in the sunroom wander

and the ancient method
of damage and repair

seems so much older than collage.

Last week I met a painter.

He recommended the ancient method
   of practicing not being a sculpture.

He said listen to records
   you have up

      these wooden stairs in milk
         crates lugged,

      and from the vinyl

      dust disturbed
         will build a dust

         in light column like those in

      a natural museum,

         or a school

      outside which imperfect
      I pledge

         allegiance to the flag
         of not only music
         can tell the truth.

         Ghost in you do you remember
            me brand-new in a used

         trenchcoat
      down the avenue striding?

Despite itself
    new wave laughed
        for it knew

    in my black
        impurities

    will always leave

        a slight trace.

    For I will always
        be devising
    some totally painless

    connector determination system
    to keep everyone from hurting.

Or waiting for
    some flower
through the kitchen window
    to climb.

    The priest below

plays creepy chanting opera music

    and up through my feet

I can feel
    him clatter among his prayers.

The scent of something extremely holy

suggests his translucent chalice
collection I never
politely

once will look through

for who knows what

I will spend
the next several
decades asleep

like a great metal wheel in the dust unlearning.

I once knew
a wooden face,

I used to visit her in a church

that did not belong to me,

uncareful she smiled
eyes shut down

on a tall ugly boy in sneakers.

I once knew a portrait
so poorly drawn

the clumsy depiction
made the face in it far more human

than any I ever actually knew.

In an afternoon

full of rented shadows

I was less afraid
for the questions
with wings

that came
        to perch
unafraid on my shoulders

                than for myself
                who had at some moment

        to care for them

    in weakness and sleep agreed.

    Someone along the ledge has taken
decades to arrange

        a row of pink yellow red and green
        colored jars through which

                I see the procession
                in celebration of worship
                in small communities such as this one

                moving beneath my window.

    Through it a girl
                in her red dress to which

her mother must have fastened

impossibly fake
giant made from a thousand

cotton balls wings

is twirling.

I wish I could hear what she's hearing.

Town hall moves
behind a cloud.

And in the sunroom all the stations
blink once again

into static and somewhere
deep in malfunction wander.

Off the scaffold workmen are leaping
into the arms of lunch.

All day with hammer claws
they yank wet shingles

and do not look at the sea.
The one you grew up by.

Troubled glass sounds.

A shadow is climbing the wall.

Good borough people,

just as the last ceremonial
    day of winter

leaves a wreath
floating on the water,

        you brought me here
    to respect relation,

            to put truth
            and beauty together

        though sometimes I tear them
        apart.

Cat Radio

All through february month of war
the eyes of the cat are pacing cats

cats hate money they shred it in millions
stalking the light from colored glass bottle

to bottle slow leaping light is winning
listen to old drama fill this room

carry on you women of athens!
don't let anyone turn on your radios!

listen to buster keaton stumble
his clubfoot toward the window to open

the window and make this room an orchestra
dispensing who cares I do static

to those who do not down on the street
know how much they need it they do

just as other rooms freelancing turn
their heads to whatever question the program

unveils like can a masterpiece be
one if it does not sleep

in a museum or linger
under the fingers of mingus

or must it be grand enough to discuss
a recipe for eggnog with the gathering

of death row exonerated
we'll be right back

we have all been for a moment
by the staggering calliope of theme music

from death exonerated
then back to the problem

of how we bend
to describe long ago or cruelty writing

the walls of the cave with whose blood
or how

spring was constructed
precisely to make us

feel like a leaf licked by a dinosaur
or mountain ranges newly parted

or others like what ever happened to me
and you who said

you would be right back
we are waiting

we are paid for in tiny bundles
of time to conjecture or solve these problems

o time of waiting I have always been
a time of waiting now it's for you

to finish your program
the stagehand says

he doesn't mind from imitation starting
it's a place at least

to start all he knows
is his memory drops

kind of away
and different times call for different pills

not being a director I don't mind
all I know is necessity

solves the problem too big for the door
big strong arms of imagination

do you know you don't know
how you dazzle by holding

the mirror and breaking
the path of sunlight

with the question that answers
dazzle my mirror

where are people wherever they go

Lazy Comet, Hurry

At the party to celebrate the party everyone
so slowed down and pretending to look
like they never once knew how just to like
tonight with more than a feeling she
comes how deep is your landslide or each
other as easy as you and I wireless live
from inside the lotus reporting this party
is not fine without us even this party
would have us believing a hotel is mostly
a place to rest a talent for situations
such as these sleepy day elevators never
reproach they forgive me strobing a front step
superflower time of waiting no wannabe
sorrow to brush my reverie I am wind
up a dress and so many questions like what
color tanktop and isn't always the oldest
thing somewhere on earth and who knew
why baltimore had a coast slaves did say
would it be too extreme to say I'm a slave
to the question what kind of music
would ever dare leave you I am a dress
you are not in saying where do you want me
supine I spun you then over then stunned
american poetry is thinking of you
do you wish I would come back and leave
you alone or take you first roughly then
to the movies in the half functioning I think
might have witnessed my first kiss with its posing
half mannequins mall or into the driveway
pulling abstracted luscious leaking the

question into my mouth how many hours
can watch me brushing the seventies
back from your secrets without me share them
only I know where you've been blazing

Kill Van Kull

How many times
can one take the ghost

      to staten island
      and still believe

one is living
and as god intended,

intentionless
      between
      two beers seated

on a plastic lip
over the known

edge of the phobic waters?

Eventually from the apartment
one must emerge

one must
outside the typewriter
skin taut inside

      exactly a t-shirt
      stand

above the avenues

wake more radiant
than a dream of radiance

of those pale in the frame
who ever with willingness

surrounded you.

You must
you will your day calm.

One must thank you
        things
        thinning the crowds

how you left us
whatever extent
unprotected

        from the decade notion:

        we are when we exempt
                ourselves exempt.

Torturers of morning
agree.

        Prose tulips   once lined

        the avenue

down which certain women

passed

 assuring over their shoulders

something
 good will happen soon,

soon the uncomfortable

shifting
 gaze on the piano bench
 will settle
 and the vase

will see

 a voice
 drop the mention

of between us
it's snowing and

thing I know
next you've taken

all my months to hide behind

your knee

the little spot
 my work ethic
 dreams away from.

Anyway long ago

      on my shoulders
        I left
          my folktale holding
      the little hiding

book I need
locked away in winterlands,

brooding
among the hurts.

Hated fathers,
keepers of the green

science notebook   you never even

enough of the dreamsands

      to let me stumble
        in love with tulip,

tulip who came
in the night and freed me

terribly from my claims

      this is not meant
      in a small room

with just a few letters
that read me aloud.

How formed we were.

Those beautiful falls

        I stood over
   holding her hand

like a child
   we were lucky

just not with morning

   where this is writing
   imagine a future
       of equally bright hours

as the one I did
with me in it.

Walk right out
   of the smoke and follow

that flower passing
under the window.

It's good to die a little.

The Book of Oxygen

I am always a house
    with nobody in it
        not the middle of winter
            not even me
        taping plastic to the windows
          to keep cold air
filling the house with sails,
        Now we're moving
         just fast enough
              on the couch to see you
                about to always
            spill
        your limbs
     a glass of syntax
   lying a little
        golden
          window
       on the tip of your tongue.
     Pass it to me.
Let's see what calibrations
     and kindnesses I am
         always in your handwriting
     rediscovering.
   Always I am
into my desk drawer
   cabinet of wanders
       wandering to rediscover
         it's snowing.
     Through it I touch
        a nail someone gave me

to hang a great task on,
say describe
a painting
you have never not walked in,
its tiny
colored
glaciers drifting
down to the floor
or something so equally
left undone.
Like a schedule
of instances
composed in red pen
and left oh for breezes
through a white barn
to do.
Antennas on hills
decreed by december's
infallible bureaucracy
deliver little
caskets of tears
are in your eyes
to be won on the radio
songs.
I hardly ever
understand the ritual.
Deliver me
everywhere
guardian spider,
guardian decade
through the leaves through me
without further election
deliver me
everywhere,

everywhere
   the radio decrees
      the transparent runaway taxi party
         inoculate the party
      of the lost domain.
       Thus I silent
     and unlike a father
      hang
       in watch
     of the hill where so full
of morning glory
    and portents you flew
        a butterfly for hours
      in the shape of a kite.
     You were hardly there
    beneath your feet.
  Undisturbed
    the grasses blew.

v

Brooklyn with a New Beginning

In the beginning the sounds of one radio
        in a window quietly passing
   a little music among the news

   of the day to another
       seemed to be the always
cantata melancholia always

   sings about how it is always
     sigh transcribing
        wind through the leaves

   and the sparrow's mechanical chirping
     into a fugue
       composed to be answered

     by the sole wooden instrument
      glued together as me.
But aleatory in the leaves

     a little prelude said
welcome don't be an asshole to morning.
   And the broken birdbath

     in the little roof garden
       not too far from the fouled Gowanus
was heard to patter a happy tune

of I'm not trying
not to teach you
something you already know.

No longer was the water three women
with slightly translucent skin
discussing something

in light autumn falling rain,
nor the blue women of troublesome creek
my friend A. once told me

live in the hollows of my blood
and cannot be cured
by injections of methylene blue.

For a long time their voices
have made a beautiful
troubling through the branches.

Recently someone's dying screenwriter brother
has rented me a late morning window full
of late morning ghosts

who watch me watching
an elm.
In early autumn appearance it runs

an already grey wrinkled hand
over the face
of a brownstone glittering in September,

alone among the furniture I walk
thinking this apartment in Brooklyn
looks out on Brooklyn

Brooklyn
Brooklyn's a row
Brooklyn's a row of dented Sundays,

full of terrible laughter
from the apartment below
where with daily rental reminders

the crackhead manager
fractures community sleep.
Afternoons in the playground

teenagers hang
on the bars,
in my window I smoke

with them and laugh
at death
and its mirror and with them practice

the oscillation method among
gradations of love and uncaring.
September every instance of

each of your elm's
small brown more than slightly
vaginal each with a flat

little wing around it
fruits to the sidewalk falling will bring
a dark green sculpture

into the world,
i.e. leaf, i.e. dearie, i.e. little bird.
Phloem necrosis, please enter

and leave me
one last siberian
elm of forget her dark hair,

move on.
Of the tree of heaven
ailanthus altissima

arbo ciela I love the name
but hate the leaves,
they smell throughout Brooklyn like urine

or sperm,
sadly a green light agrees,
at 30 they die

and shaped like umbrellas
or vases the crowns
of the majestic elms make fun

of how sunlight through
the tree of heaven
dribbles down to the ground.

Ailanthus tree that's a weed
pathetic like a fallacy
halfway through my life

I live next to the community garden.
Above it your branches
wave a little against the sky,

casting pale green shadows
upon the gardeners.
I have seen

great metal wings of the storm king
swivel in wind and bow
to solitude in a field.

In the rented room I have watched
a film begin
with monks who follow

whatever figure ignores them,
and end with failure
in a white suit smiling.

At night my ideas
sometimes glowed
a little and were manageable glowing units,

it was unclear whether
the glow was reflection
or as in a lantern made of white paper

came from within,
or if to continue such decipherment
contributes detracts

or is itself the enactment of
the aesthetics of bioluminescence.
By the light of one paper lantern I've drunk

seltzer with lemon in the dark.
I've asked docent of night
of the sunken beneath the water cathedral

who knows
who knows where the sparrow falls?
Aloud I said sometimes a bomb

shows a certain
precise concern.
Let's pass the night

discussing for whom.
Let's pass the night discussing if
I've ever felt anything true.

Blue accuses morning of birds.
It's enough
to try to be beautiful.

A woman's lover
from a hotel named for a painter
has out into night

in search of experience wandered.
　　　　Below her he stands
not seeing her watching

him pause to listen to a bell
　　　outline a particular
attitude toward the promise of night

　　　　　　then hop on his moped.
　　From a window
a girl waves down at the street

while rain like a lover arrives.
　　For too long I have gone
　　　cycladic to sit

an island in afternoon's sea
　　　staring at the harpist
carved from white stone,

the one you could fit in a hand.
　　　　Gently he's always
　　about to touch

tiny white polished nails
　　attached to white hands
　　　　　　fashioned as crudely

　　as those of an infant
　to the mute strings.
There is a discretion in stone that I envy.

It does not say
you should not live
only in a museum.

Blue is the color my eyes become
when looking into
my blue notebook with a blue dragonfly

etched in darker blue on the cover.
Blue are they when I'm asleep
or looking down.

Blue was the sea
long ago when it said
you've been chosen

to be like everyone else,
and because you do not know
I will throw

your bathing suit above your ears
and your ass like a white desperate
flag of surrender

to cruel adolescence
on the beach with its mysterious
evening firelight gatherings.

Blue are they now
when I thank the I think
dominican noise

situation for its extra
phrases I borrow and never return.
The breeze

leans a certain
        always watchful
playground against a twisted bike

        and enters this room
full of shadows to blow
out the match

        of what I've been thinking
when no one else is around.

More Trees

From each I've climbed
a little less perfect
down a little more clumsy
in carrying
what I don't know.
How to walk
with a limp that conceals
no suffering.
How to wave in spring
and dismiss it
too soon.
How if I don't
hold still
anything at all
can drift
into my hand
that destroyer.
How if I wave
the other crooked
true finger knows
I should have been taught
or just known
the shy air conditioner
in our window sailed
all the way from
California
that destroyer
E. you said it
stars never glitter
like money, stars

are mere and accept
our praise precisely
so we don't with our grace
disturb them.
Never write about trees,
agreed my friend and I.
Let's agree on porchlight
my friend and I agreed,
hurtling back down
into each other
the city overlooked.
It was always
a tuesday the city
overlooked a playground
climbing all over
the children, small
hands in big ones
say go learning
to walk hand
in no one's hand
to the school of
outside the classroom
crying, your nose
just seems to bleed
for no reason,
one wants not to be
by oneself alone,
one wants ice, one
wants pressure,
one wants not to hear
another reading
they are readying
in the times,

go piercing
the buildings say,
placid the buildings
lean down collapsing
must we collapse
for you to go
from your shell you shadow
of porchlight who
did not
what he must
but he should
believing into the dictionary
of tree heads below
where a light among leaves
I am
above me
and known
to let me linger.

What I Need

Sometimes only a bridge
through the clouds.
Sometimes to be silent.
Sometimes slow vane
to learn your skills.
Stoops of Philadelphia teach
constitutional law by halting
a moment for us
a big red one
with brick streets
cigarettes and iron trees
to talk to each other
if others are so inclined.
Due to a conference
on the role of role-playing
in organizations
for raising funds
I am wandering the capital
of our early nation.
In the hotel room
on a metallic eyebrow
I cut my hand,
the body of summer
was huge, by the window
with my antenna I was
unlocked catching
fields of wireless.
Due to a system error
the application June
unexpectedly quit.
Due to a region of lakes

an orange cat narrows
his eyes and licks
my hand then wanders
back into the future to sleep
on a tag-sale couch
you will buy so sunbeam
on the edge of winter can read
a little Ishiguro, climb
my face, then a mountain
in a picture you took.
For its museum
of natural history
the early capital is known.
It's more like a cabinet
of wonders organized
by scientists frantic
at the prospect of science,
a museum of natural wandering.
To learn about science
here you must make
wander a method
and from that method
be willing even to wander.
On the wall of a replica
of a laboratory
where so children can
without experimenting
experiment nothing works
a movie flickers.
Day 42, the chicks
are once again ready to hatch,
the children are
once again yawning
clapping and slinging their packs

over one shoulder.
From the museum they stream
into the same yellow buses
we streamed into
when we were children.
Into when we were children
I often stream
and think of which thing
could have been different.
Not the yellow bus
waiting for me outside the museum
where the pendulum
slowly knocked over its pins.
Poor pendulum proving.
Poor tattered flag
breathed upon by so many
children with mouths poorly brushed
you have not enough stars.
Now you have been restored,
and behind some glass
cling to a couple
of atoms of Betsy Ross.
While I was dreaming
the children have gone.
I missed yet again
evening arriving
to sit on its bench in the park.
Like a cyborg
it does not know
why it makes
origami with shadows of leaves
nor why it is happy
we think of it
sometimes as a person.

At night the lamps
come automatically on.
This is always
somewhat unexpected,
like a picture I hand
of when you are happy
to you. With my hand
lifted slightly I slowed
the trains, back into
the crook of my arm
you fell lunar
and heavy and dreamed.
When something small
that does what scientists
consider useful
comes to change everything
what will we do?
Still asleep you woke
to tell me
perhaps it will not.
Much later I found
a map on your shoulder.

Ancient Sorrow Sleep Already

It takes a great act of will to poke your head
out of the nocturnes to say those clouds
might seem to be hanging but fact is Emily
was just being careful enough and you must
collide at least once in your teens
so better some slow debacle with a willow
better to flatten a mirthless fence
while its father emits a small overdetermined
ball of laughter refusing to pop
in your throat until a girl with her own
small bird in hers makes of your story
a sleep nest in her chest and knows
better an ambulance followed by an ambulance
for whoever heard such a thing in a story
do they do that always or only on weekends
do you bruise most to know most things you grasp
you cannot sometimes silence without any wishing
is best for others on the phone
like I'd like to purchase you something
you wouldn't notice but won't I was thinking
perhaps a replica of your house so without it
in any way impacting them guests and calamities
could be savored by you and Jim impervious
though I suppose that's what's known
as a poor idea and what could we do
about Rita no way to duplicate her quantumly
complex compact among eagerness anger
and rolling on her back to duplicate
such a pleasure would be for you cruel

as removing the way you so gracefully cede
a portion of silence that it may regard
itself inside someone shoeless hunched
over The Agony of Flies in your kitchen
eating too much gumbo and raveling
awkward theories of how one constructs
a system of ethics from the words not ghosts
but ether itself forms in ouija and suddenly
everyone knows you mean scrabble and feels
all the more kindly toward you
so why not agree we had a choice
to allow it to continue just as anyway
why not instead a big bright day
your garden can hang like a mirror reflecting
ideas like a friend sits you down in a time
you are not usually sat down in a bar and says
friend and suddenly you are with him
constructing a chrysalis that will survive
long after the small pain formed inside it
has gone on to become
famous for saying friend I've struggled
a long time to tell you this

Andale Mono

Today I walked past my door in the rain
and put an old key
in a lock from which gold light shone.
Gold light through the keyhole like didactic
material below a painting glows to explain
the nineteenth century and other things we must know.
In the poem we want to try to set off a light each time
the door of the closet is closed. And to be
for the reader a mechanism attached to a string
the poem pulls. And piecing together
as desperately as we can. By fragments we mean
pieces of things we thought we have heard,
and when we say them mean though we cannot
see you we love you. By light we mean light.
Fear is a mechanism thinking too much
and not enough about the closet
holding something. The light in the closet
is on, the garments are thinking,
the door to the closet opens
into a long empty corridor we fear
for verily it like a torch
in the british sense through a dusty room
pervades us. When we are walking
with our torch meaning flashlight before us
reaching for the long poem inside us
one door explains how to read for both meaning
and pleasure. Another shuts.
The poem Andale Mono begins.
When I was a child I used to give speeches
into the mouth of the dishwasher open and gleaming.

When in a private language I said
ritual laughter mother and father
without knowing commit transmits
a kind of anger it understood,
though they were not.
Today I walked right past the face of a woman
I was sure was in Andale Mono.
Today I walked right past the poem
I knew and looked
into a lake which is now my wife.
My wife has entered the room. She is
a finger lake. In one hand she is holding
a sweater, pink, in the other a cream colored
spatula. *Which one do you like best?*
The poem is now my wife. For the first time
today in Andale Mono I drew my shoulders
back and looked straight forward and slightly
up. All day for the first time things were
true size. Droplets hung from my lashes
strobing at times the warehouse
next to the elevated, at others the brand-new
cathedral from which small people were streaming,
lugging large black musical instrument cases.
Large black chambers hold the delicate
wooden chambers for making chamber music.
In Andale Mono things are both breakable
and strong. In Andale Mono just out of reach
of my dangling hand the lock was a tiny door.

About the Author

Matthew Zapruder was born in 1967 in Washington, D.C. He is the author of one previous book of poetry, *American Linden* (Tupelo Press, 2002), and is the co-translator of Romanian poet Eugen Jebeleanu's final collection, *Secret Weapon* (Coffee House, 2007). He lives in New York City, where he works as an editor for Wave Books and teaches poetry in the M.F.A. Program in Creative Writing at the New School University.

Copper Canyon Press wishes to acknowledge the support of Lannan Foundation in funding the publication and distribution of exceptional literary works.

LANNAN LITERARY SELECTIONS 2006

Madeline DeFrees, *Spectral Waves*
Taha Muhammad Ali, *So What: New & Selected Poems*
Theodore Roethke, *Straw for the Fire: From the Notebooks of Theodore Roethke*
Benjamin Alire Sáenz, *Dreaming the End of War*
Matthew Zapruder, *The Pajamaist*

LANNAN LITERARY SELECTIONS 2000–2005

Marvin Bell, *Rampant*

Hayden Carruth, *Doctor Jazz*

Cyrus Cassells, *More Than Peace and Cypresses*

Norman Dubie, *The Mercy Seat: Collected & New Poems, 1967–2001*

Sascha Feinstein, *Misterioso*

James Galvin, *X: Poems*

Jim Harrison, *The Shape of the Journey: New and Collected Poems*

Hồ Xuân Hương, *Spring Essence: The Poetry of Hồ Xuân Hương,* translated by John Balaban

June Jordan, *Directed by Desire: The Collected Poems of June Jordan*

Maxine Kumin, *Always Beginning: Essays on a Life in Poetry*

Ben Lerner, *The Lichtenberg Figures*

Antonio Machado, *Border of a Dream: Selected Poems,* translated by Willis Barnstone

W.S. Merwin, *The First Four Books of Poems, Migration: New & Selected Poems, Present Company*

Pablo Neruda, *The Separate Rose, Still Another Day,* translated by William O'Daly

Cesare Pavese, *Disaffections: Complete Poems 1930–1950,* translated by Geoffrey Brock

Antonio Porchia, *Voices,* translated by W.S. Merwin

Kenneth Rexroth, *The Complete Poems of Kenneth Rexroth*

Alberto Ríos, *The Smallest Muscle in the Human Body, The Theater of Night*

Theodore Roethke, *On Poetry & Craft: Selected Prose of Theodore Roethke*

Ann Stanford, *Holding Our Own: The Selected Poems of Ann Stanford*

Ruth Stone, *In the Next Galaxy*

Joseph Stroud, *Country of Light*

Rabindranath Tagore, *The Lover of God,* translated by Tony K. Stewart and Chase Twichell

Reversible Monuments: Contemporary Mexican Poetry, edited by Mónica de la Torre and Michael Wiegers

César Vallejo, *The Black Heralds,* translated by Rebecca Seiferle

Eleanor Rand Wilner, *The Girl with Bees in Her Hair*

C.D. Wright, *Steal Away: Selected and New Poems*

The Chinese character for poetry is made up of two parts: "word" and "temple." It also serves as pressmark for Copper Canyon Press.

Founded in 1972, Copper Canyon Press remains dedicated to publishing poetry exclusively, from Nobel laureates to new and emerging authors. The Press thrives with the generous patronage of readers, writers, book-sellers, librarians, teachers, students, and funders—everyone who shares the conviction that poetry invigorates the language and sharpens our appreciation of the world.

Major funding has been provided by:

Anonymous (2)
The Paul G. Allen Family Foundation
Lannan Foundation
National Endowment for the Arts
Washington State Arts Commission

For information and catalogs:

COPPER CANYON PRESS
Post Office Box 271
Port Townsend, Washington 98368
360-385-4925
www.coppercanyonpress.org